WILD ANIMALS OF THE NORTH

Dieter Braun

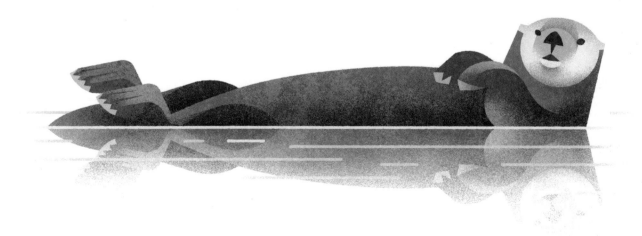

Flying Eye Books
London - New York

Wild Animals of the North

It's hard to imagine that fantastic creatures like bald eagles or snow leopards could have evolved from the first single-celled organisms that appeared on Earth around 3.5 billion years ago. Today, many millions of diverse species populate our planet. Some of them are absolutely tiny, others are truly enormous; they have feathers, scales, or fur; they are one colour or many colours; with or without vertebrae, with fins, wings, antennae or paws – in short: the richness of our wildlife is immeasurably vast. However, there are fewer and fewer species in the wild as humans intrude further into their habitats. Pollution and climate change also pose a threat to many species. The most well known example is perhaps that of the majestic polar bear: the pack ice is literally melting away from under its paws due to global warming. Almost a third of the animals in this book are endangered and some are even threatened with extinction. Even if mankind can go on without them, a piece of our vibrantly diverse world dies along with each species.

This book takes us on a journey to the farthest corners of the northern hemisphere. We will dive with great dolphins to the depths of the ocean, burrow through the undergrowth with wild boar, trot across the dry steppes with two-humped camels and climb high mountain peaks with the markhor. We'll pay the arctic fox a visit in the freezing cold of Siberia, watch the pileated woodpecker foraging for food and keep the rare Iberian lynx company in the shimmering heat of Spain.

Have fun in the wilderness!

EUROPE
// REGION 2

NORTH AMERICA
// REGION 1

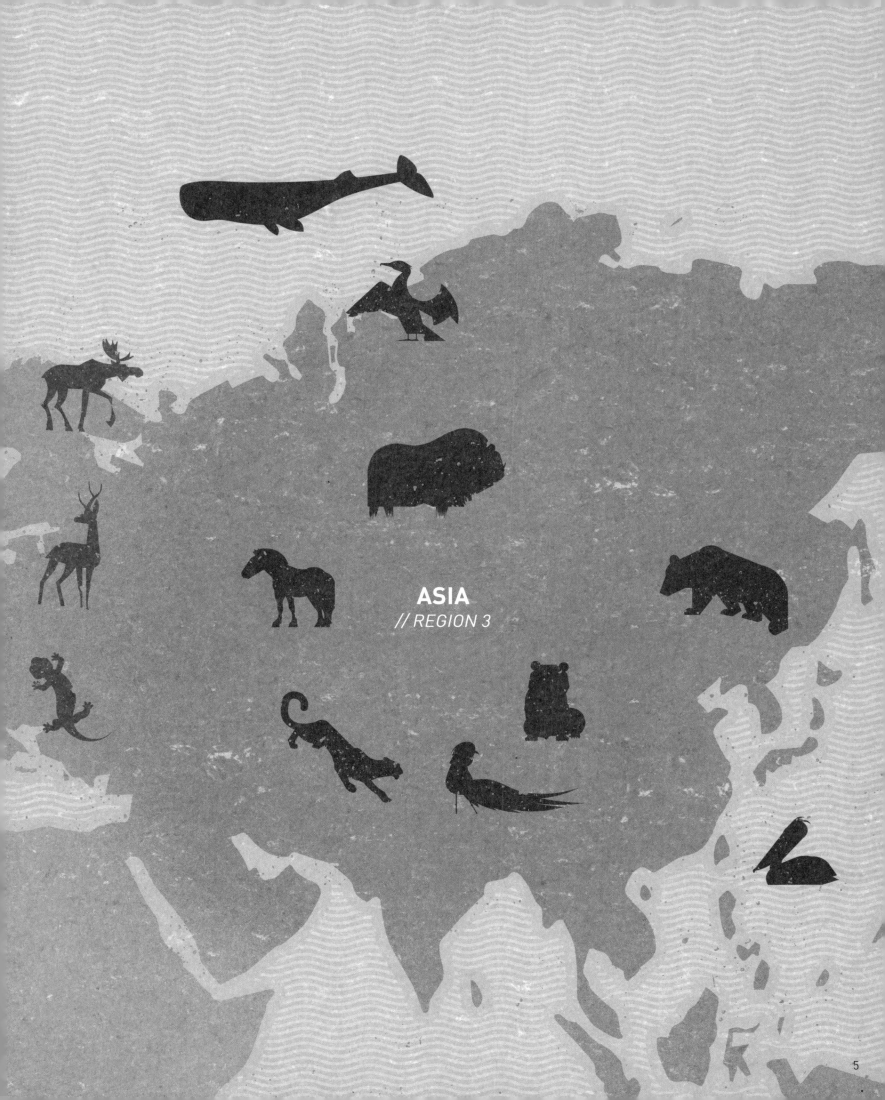

ASIA
// REGION 3

REGION 1

NORTH AMERICA

Puma // *Puma concolor*

The light brown puma goes by many names: the silver lion, the mountain lion, or the cougar. Measuring up to 1.4 metres in length, it's one of the largest big cats in North America. The further north you go, the bigger the puma will be! Scientists, however, still class it as a small cat, just like its cousin the African cheetah.
It may be hard to believe, but the mountain lion is more closely related to the domestic cat than it is to the lion: just like cats, pumas can retract their claws, are extremely agile, and can make a standing jump of up to five metres into a tree.

Bald Eagle // *Haliaeetus leucocephalus*

Every child in the USA knows the bald eagle – it's the national emblem of the United States of America. Few animals are as majestic as these mighty birds of prey, and their homes are just as impressive. These masters of the sky build their nests, more commonly known as eyries, at high altitudes and preferably in the treetops. Their nests have been known to weigh tonnes because an eagle will continually build it. Every year the eagle adds more twigs and branches until the bird's nest eventually becomes too heavy and collapses. The love between two eagles, on the other hand, lasts a lifetime.

Kodiak Bear // *Ursus arctos middendorffi*

The Kodiak bear lives on Kodiak Island and the surrounding islands of South Alaska. The polar bear excluded, the Kodiak bear is the largest land-dwelling carnivore in the world. They can grow up to three metres in length and weigh almost 800 kilogrammes. As omnivores they often content themselves with plants, berries or roots, but carrion can also be on the menu. A very special feast awaits the Kodiak bear in summer and autumn when the salmon migrate to breed. The bears position themselves at small waterfalls and simply wait for the bite-sized salmon to jump right into their mouths!

Mountain Goat // *Oreamnos americanus*

Orca // *Orcinus orca*

Orcas, also known as grampus, belong to the dolphin family and are among
the biggest carnivores in the world. They are at the top of the food chain in
their habitat, which means they don't have any natural predators that could
put them in any real danger. Orcas are also known as 'Killer Whales,' but
'Whale Killers' would be a better name; other kinds of whales and small
dolphins are part of their diet. Orcas live together in groups and each family
has its own dialect that they use to communicate.

Polar Bear // *Ursus maritimus*

Native to the northern polar region, polar bears are the largest land-dwelling carnivores in the world. They are also in their element in the water as they are excellent long distance swimmers and can travel five kilometres an hour, but prefer to hunt their prey on land. Different kinds of seals and young or weakened walruses should be wary when the 'white giant' is hungry. Incidentally, its coat is not strictly speaking white: it only appears that way because of the reflection of the sun. The hairs of its outer coat are actually hollow and translucent and the skin underneath is black.

Seal // *Phoca vitulina*

Blue-Footed Booby // *Sula nebouxii*

What makes the blue-footed booby so special is
– of course – its beautiful blue feet. But why are
they blue? There are two reasons: firstly, there are
collagen fibres between the webbing of its feet, which
predominantly reflect blue light. Secondly, the booby
consumes a blue pigment via its food, which is what
gives it its blue legs and feet. The females choose
partners with the bluest feet because they are an
indicator that the male will always bring the tastiest
of morsels back to the nest.

Wolf // *Canis lupus*

Few animals have inspired as many stories and legends as the wolf. You might have read the story of the big bad wolf who gobbled up the little girl and her beloved grandmother, and perhaps been told the myth of the lone wolf. In reality, the wolf needs to fear humans, who have eradicated it from many of its original habitats. Wolves are also very rarely alone. They usually live in family groups, called packs, which have a clear social structure with high-ranking and low-ranking members.

Chipmunks // *Tamias*

Grey Squirrel // *Sciurus carolinensis*

Bison // *Bison*

American Lobster // *Homarus americanus*

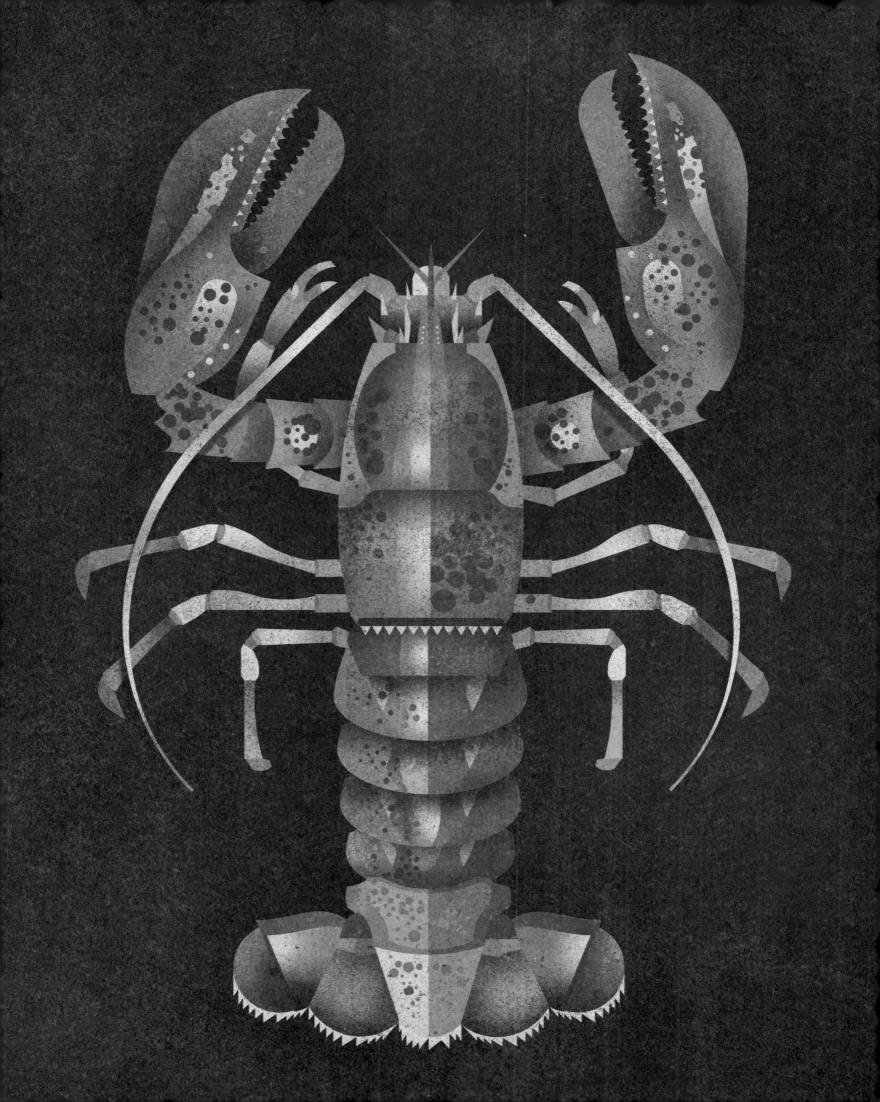

Monarch Butterfly // *Danaus plexippus*

Isn't it incredible that some animals can completely change shape over the course of their lifetime? This transformation is called metamorphosis. The monarch butterfly begins life as an egg, from which a caterpillar hatches. The caterpillar can be identified by its typical white, black and yellow patterned body. When it is older and full from feeding, the caterpillar rests and the pupal stage begins. After a while, a beautiful butterfly hatches from the light green cocoon – a kind of sleeping bag – and flies off to start its new life.

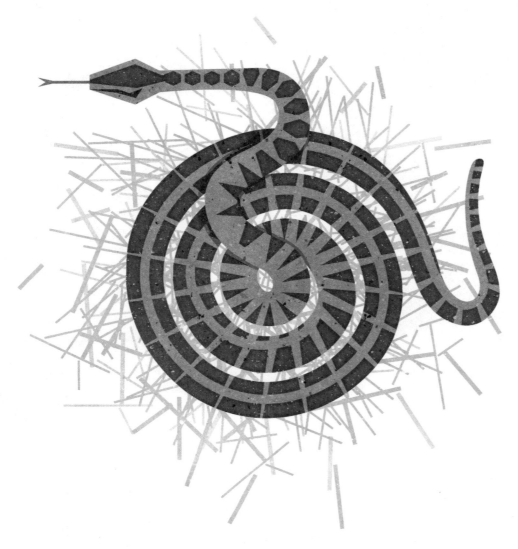

Texas Rattlesnake // *Crotalus atrox*

Rattling is a skill every rattlesnake possesses. When it feels
threatened it produces a rattling noise with the overlapping thorny
scales on the end of its tale – the so-called rattle. If this warning
signal isn't enough to deter predators, the snake is highly poisonous
and can bite. At up to two metres in length, the Texas Rattlesnake is
one of the largest rattlesnakes in the world and as such produces a
large amount of poison. Because the mother incubates her young
inside her body, they come into the world fully active.

Coyote // *Canis latrans*

Sea Otter // *Enhydra lutris*

Elk // *Cervus canadensis*

Long-Tailed Duck // *Clangula hyemalis*

These sociable ducks' chatty nature was once likened to the friendly talk of the local native Inuit tribe. The ducks' call has the reputation of being the most melodious in the whole of the duck world. The males distinguish themselves from the brown-black females with their black and white plumage and extended tail. Long-tailed ducks are excellent divers and when foraging for food they can go to depths of up to sixty metres.

King Eider // *Somateria spectabilis*

Striped Skunk // *Mephitis mephitis*

The striped skunk is a stinker in the truest sense of the word. The almost odourless animal has the ability to produce a pungent substance using its anal glands. When threatened by a predator – usually a bird of prey – it puts its backside in the air, lifts its bushy tail and attempts to spray an attacker, up to three metres away, in the face with the stinking secretion. Even the hungriest bird of prey would surely have imagined a delicious meal to be something quite different.

Pronghorn Antelope // *Antilocapra americana*

Raccoon // *Procyon lotor*

Raccoons are true finger acrobats. Everything they can get their paws on is lifted, rotated, turned over and meticulously scrutinised – it can sometimes look like the animals want to clean their discoveries. The indigenous Algonquian people named this small nocturnal bear 'arakun', which when translated means something like 'he who scratches with his hands'. When a raccoon finds something delicious to eat it gorges itself to bursting. In order to withstand the icy winter, the raccoon eats so much food that its weight increases by up to fifty percent.

Reindeer // *Rangifer tarandus*

Canadian Beaver // *Castor canadensis*

Beavers are the masters of building lodges and dams. Their front paws, which they can skilfully use to grasp and build with, perfectly equip them for these tasks. They have a waterproof coat and webbed toes on their hind paws and spend almost their entire lives in the water. Their board-shaped, club-like tail provides additional control for when the beaver embarks upon its diving manoeuvres. However, its most important tool is its strong incisors. The beaver gnaws building materials – twigs and branches – into shape and can even bite through trees a metre in diameter to build its beaver lodge.

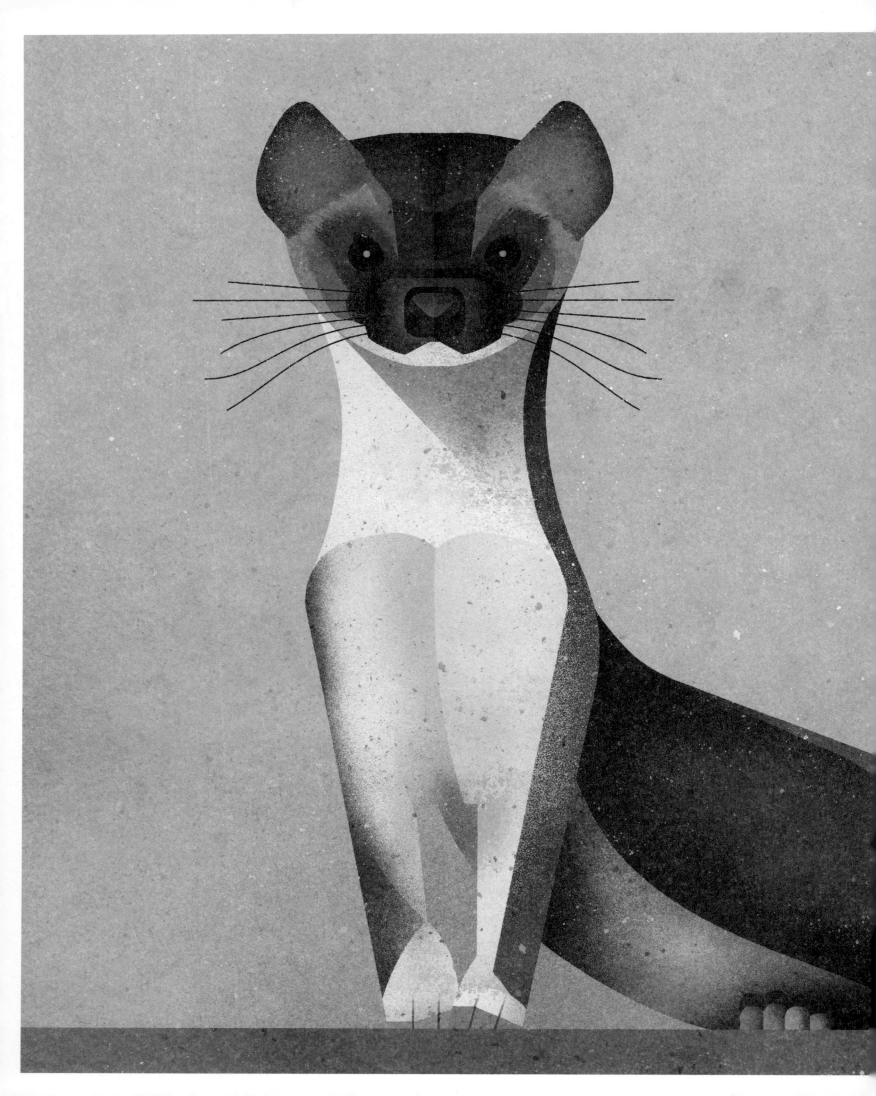

Long-Tailed Weasel // *Mustela frenata*

The long-tailed weasel knows that clothes make the man, so its fur adapts for every season: in summer its back is brown and its belly is cream, while in winter a white fur covers its long, slender body. Its year-round trademark is a stylish black accent on the tip of its tail. Agile and elegant, these skilful hunters can squeeze into the tightest of animal burrows. Apart from mice and small rabbits, birds and reptiles are also on the weasel's menu.

Turkey // *Meleagris gallopavo*

Pileated Woodpecker // *Dryocopus pileatus*

The woodpecker is the carpenter of the bird kingdom. Its only tool for den building is its beak. The pileated woodpecker pecks up to 12,000 times a day on solid wood without getting a headache – its skull is specially designed for this extreme work. The pecking or tapping isn't just for housebuilding, but also for searching for food. This sound also loudly marks out its hunting ground and gets the attention of female woodpeckers. The finished nesting hole high up in the trees is where the offspring are brought up. Once the young have left, the nest is given over to another grateful tenant – this might be another bird, but may also be a small mammal or reptile.

Walrus // *Odobenus rosmarus*

What does it take to be the chief of a walrus clan? The longest tusks, of course – that's what the two protruding canines of a walrus are called. These long teeth are not only used to heave the walrus across the rocks, but also to make holes in the ice for its next diving trip. However, the walrus mainly uses its tusks as weapons against its predators: the polar bear and the orca. A polar bear can fatally injure a walrus. The long tusks aren't as practical while foraging – this is where its beard hairs come in handy for catching mussels and crabs.

Puffin // *Fratercula arctica*

REGION 2
EUROPE

Red Fox // *Vulpes vulpes*

When a fox sneaks gracefully towards its favourite prey and makes a so-called 'mouse jump', it brings to mind a cat rather than a canid – a canine predator – which is what it is classed as. Even its diet is significantly different to that of a dog or a wolf. The fox predominantly drags small animals like mice, rabbits and partridges into its den, but once in a while it will also eat earthworms and frogs. It rounds out its diet with delicious fruits, like raspberries and plums.

Compass Jellyfish // *Chrysaora hysoscella*

Grey Heron // *Ardea cinerea*

Roe Deer // *Capreolus capreolus*

The roe deer is the smallest and most common kind of deer found in Europe. The fawn – the newborn deer – is distinguished by its pretty white spots, which fade after four weeks and disappear completely with the arrival of the young deer's winter coat at the end of autumn. Most of the time, the little one is well hidden in high grass waiting for the doe – the mother – to come by and suckle it. Mother and child locate one another by making quiet whimpering sounds. Fawns have no scent of their own, so they are safe from predators like foxes or badgers, who hunt with their sense of smell.

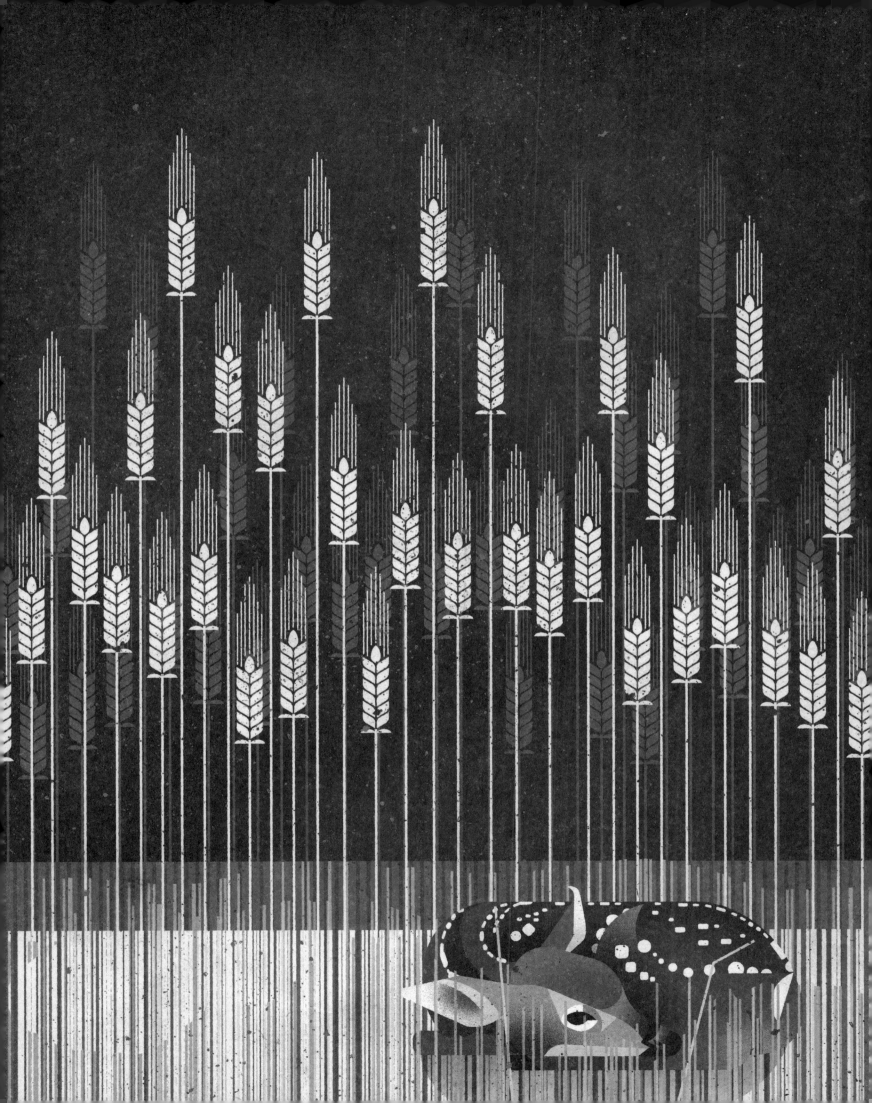

Barn Owl // *Tyto alba*

When night falls, the barn owl awakens and hunts for its favourite meal: shrews and field mice. Its pair of extraordinary eyes and its impressive hearing help it hunt in the deep black night. This is how it can see the slightest of movements made by a mouse on the ground even under a thick layer of snow. When two barn owls find one another, they stay together for life. Their heart shaped faces must be a sign of their faithful souls!

Squirrel // *Sciurus vulgaris*

European Badger // *Meles Meles*

The European badger is the largest marten in central Europe. Its most characteristic feature is the black stripes running from its nose, over its eyes to its ears, and across its otherwise white head. The badger is a champion builder. With long claws on its front paws it can dig up to five-metre-deep burrows with multiple entrances. Its home is comprised of a complicated system of corridors inhabited by a family of badgers and can be extended from generation to generation. Every now and again the family of badgers tolerate a fox as a lodger whenever one makes itself comfortable in one of the cosy chambers.

White Stork // *Ciconia ciconia*

When two storks meet, a typical ritual for them is to clatter their beaks together. Storks' voices are so weak that this is the way they communicate with one another, and it is also how they have earned the nickname 'rattle stork'. It is said that the white stork delivers babies. According to legend, it brings them in bundles to human mothers or lets them slide down the chimney. This story might have come from the habit of storks nesting on chimneys and roofs to incubate their own offspring. They like to keep close to human settlements so they can always find food nearby.

Hedgehog // *Erinaceus europaeus*

Most mammals take to their heels at the first sign of danger, but not the hedgehog – its legs are too short to make a swift getaway. Instead, its strategy is to roll itself into a prickly ball to make it as unattractive as possible to its attacker. Through a complex interplay of muscles, it makes its quills stand upright. A circular muscle ensures that all unprotected parts of the body disappear under the spikey haircut. There are around 6,000 spikes on an adult hedgehog, and they are in fact modified hairs.

Wild Boar // *Sus scrofa*

White Swan // *Cygnus olor*

Black Swan // *Cygnus atratus*

Fire Salamander // *Salamandra salamandra*

A particularly beautiful amphibian is the fire salamander. Its glowing yellow spots on its shiny black skin make it a real eye-catcher, and each one has a different pattern. The fire salamander is a die-hard forest-dweller. They're mainly found in deciduous forests – if you manage to find them at all. It's only in rain or fog and preferably at night, when humans are hidden away, that the fire salamander comes out of hiding and is in its element. This is why in some regions it has other lovely names like 'little rain man' or 'rain newt'.

Iberian Lynx // *Lynx pardinus*

The Iberian lynx is a true rabbit connoisseur – it likes to eat one every day. Having to chase after one, however, is not his thing. It prefers to lie in wait for hours until its prey gets so close that it can catch it in a few determined leaps. The Iberian lynx is much smaller than its Eurasian relative, but makes up for its size by wearing its distinctive sideburns a little longer. The characteristic paintbrush hairs on its ears heighten its hearing and navigating capabilities.

Peregrine Falcon // *Falco peregrinus*

The peregrine falcon holds many records. One is that it's the fastest bird in the world: it can travel at up to 300 kilometres per hour to capture its prey – small to medium birds – which it can catch mid-flight. Another is that it's the most prevalent species of bird on earth. It is not only found in Europe, but on all other continents apart from the Antarctic. The life expectancy of a peregrine falcon is fifteen years.

European Mouflon // *Ovis orientalis musimon*

Great Spotted Woodpecker // *Dendrocopos major Syn Picoides major*

Brown Hare // *Lepus europaeus*

Wood Grouse // *Tetrao urogallus*

Red Deer // *Cervus elaphus*

The king of the forest needs his mighty antlers to intimidate the competition during mating season, but every year he gets a new crown. In the spring he discards these old bones and a new pair grows over the next hundred days. During this time, his antlers are too soft to be used as a weapon. This doesn't bother the red deer too much though, as outside of the mating season this great ruminant is a rather peace-loving fellow.

European Bison // *Bison bonasus*

Northern Bald Ibis // *Geronticus eremita*

When searching for a mate the iridescent black ibis use their Mediterranean charm to its full potential. With their splayed crest and raucous croaking, the males and females alike bow to one another several times. Through this ritual the future mate is chivalrously presented with the individual pattern on the other's bald head. And because socialising is such a priority for the crested ibis, the whole ibis colony takes part in the ritual at the same time. After all, the best way for the ibis to pair up is among its peers.

Moose // *Alces alces*

With a shoulder height of up to 2.3 metres and a body length of up to three metres, the moose is counted among the largest variety of deer on earth. The shoulders and chests of the males are especially muscular in order for them to be able to carry their immense shovel antlers. Moose are hunted by bears and wolves, but mostly without success. An adult moose can toss a wolf with its antlers or incapacitate it with a targeted kick of its hooves. It's not for nothing that the scientific name of the moose comes from the Greek word 'alce', which can mean 'power' and 'strength'.

Crane // *Grus grus*

REGION 3
ASIA

Snow Leopard // *Panthera uncia*

A snow leopard never roars. Its call is a drawn-out howl which – depending on the direction of the wind – can be mistaken for the cry of the yeti. Because it's so shy and rare, the Kyrgyz people also call it the 'ghost of the mountain'. Its long bushy tail gives this avid climber the necessary counterbalance it requires for scaling the mountainside. When resting, it uses its tail to protect itself from the cold by curling it around itself and covering its nose. It is said to jump over 15-metre crevasses – and even if the crevasse were a few centimetres shorter, this cat would still be the world champion long-jumper of all mammals.

Giant Panda // *Ailuropoda melanoleuca*

Even if pandas look like big teddy bears they belong in the predator category. In the course of evolution, however, they've largely renounced their consumption of meat and now eat almost exclusively bamboo. As this diet isn't rich in nutrients, they busy themselves for up to twelve hours a day munching as much as thirty kilogrammes of the plant. This corresponds to thirty percent of their bodyweight. Their distinctive wide head is also down to the panda's diet, because in order to feed it requires a very strong jaw and the largest molars of all predators.

Japanese Macaque // *Macaca fuscata*

These red-faced monkeys are cunning masters of adaption: due to having the coldest habitat of all primates – humans not included – they like to spend hours splashing around in Japan's hot springs to regulate their body temperature. Young monkeys learn the art of 'snowball rolling' from their peers early on. It doesn't give them any survival benefits, but it does give them an illustrative nickname: the Japanese snow monkey.

Great Black Cormorant // *Phalacrocorax carbo*

Red Panda // *Ailurus fulgens*

Musk Deer // *Moschidae*

These little deer have no antlers, but they do have a pair of handsome, vampire-like canines, which they mainly use to instil respect in their rivals during rutting. It is also during this time that they mark their territory with a strong-smelling substance from their infamous musk glands. Incidentally, they're the only deer flexible enough to easily climb trees right up into the treetops.

Yak // *Bos mutus*

Golden Pheasant // *Chrysolophus pictus*

The golden pheasant, regarded in Ancient China as a symbol for prosperity, happiness and beauty, is quite a secretive creature. Even though you couldn't find a pheasant with a more striking plumage, you can hardly ever see it in the great outdoors. This is because it never ventures out into open terrain and spends most nights in trees. This pheasant also has the reputation of being a master at detecting danger early and can vanish into thin air when it needs to.

Przewalski's Horse // *Equus ferus przewalskii*

The Mongols call these shy animals 'takhis', meaning 'spirit', and they are the only horse breed to have survived to this day in their wild variety. In contrast to the domestic horse, they not only change the fur on their body, black-booted legs and snout every year, they also change the hair on their upstanding mane. And apart from the fact that they have two chromosomes and one rib more than their relatives, there's also one more important difference: they can't be ridden.

Dalmatian Pelican // *Pelecanus crispus*

Generally, pelicans are one of the largest flying birds on earth, and the Dalmatian Pelican – with its wingspan of up to three and a half metres wide – is the biggest of them all. Its massive weight – around 13 kilogrammes – doesn't make it easy for the pelican to soar, so it requires quite a run-up before it can take off. Once in the air, however, it can fly for 24 hours non-stop. It scoops up fish almost exclusively into its throat pouch and in order to get the required kilo it needs per day, it occasionally works with other Dalmatian pelicans. Together the birds force the fish into shallow water to make them easier to catch. Preferred hunting formation: the horseshoe.

Asian Black Bear // *Ursus thibetanus*

Saiga // *Saiga tatarica*

Markhor // *Capra falconeri*

The wild relative of the domestic goat is a terrific climber. In the barren landscape, markhors effortlessly climb to places other herbivores aren't able to reach. To get the very best leaves, they may even climb trees. Their powerful, spiralled horns can grow up to one and a half metres long on some bucks.

Arctic Fox // *Vulpes lagopus*

Alpine Hare // *Lepus timidus*

Ermine // *Mustela erminea*

Mandarin Duck // *Aix galericulata*

Golden Monkey // *Rhinopithecus roxellana*

Since it's quite chilly in the mountainous provinces of central China, this blue-faced monkey wears his hair a little longer than other primates. The hair on the older males grows up to half a metre in length and warms the animal as if it were wearing a golden fur coat. In the summer they roam their forested land in unusually large hordes of up to six hundred animals.

Bottlenose Dolphin // *Tursiops truncatus*

Bottlenose dolphins are extremely clever, curious and playful. They like to cavort in the bow waves of ships or large whales, making metre-high jumps and smacking the water with their wide tail fin, better known as a fluke. Because they're also extremely social, they usually form schools with other dolphins and sometimes even accept sharks or turtles into their swimming classes.

Camel // *Camelus ferus*

Drought, sandstorms and – even worse – temperature fluctuations from -30 to +40 °C make the camel's habitat very demanding. But they have some tricks up their sleeve: they can go for days without drinking and then drink 150 litres in one go; they can close up their nostrils against dust; they can store fat reserves in their humps and use it for energy when there's nothing to eat; and they can increase their body temperature by up to 8 °C so as not to sweat too quickly.

Manul // *Otocolobus manul*

Japanese Serow // *Capricornis crispus*

Mouflon // *Ovis orientalis*

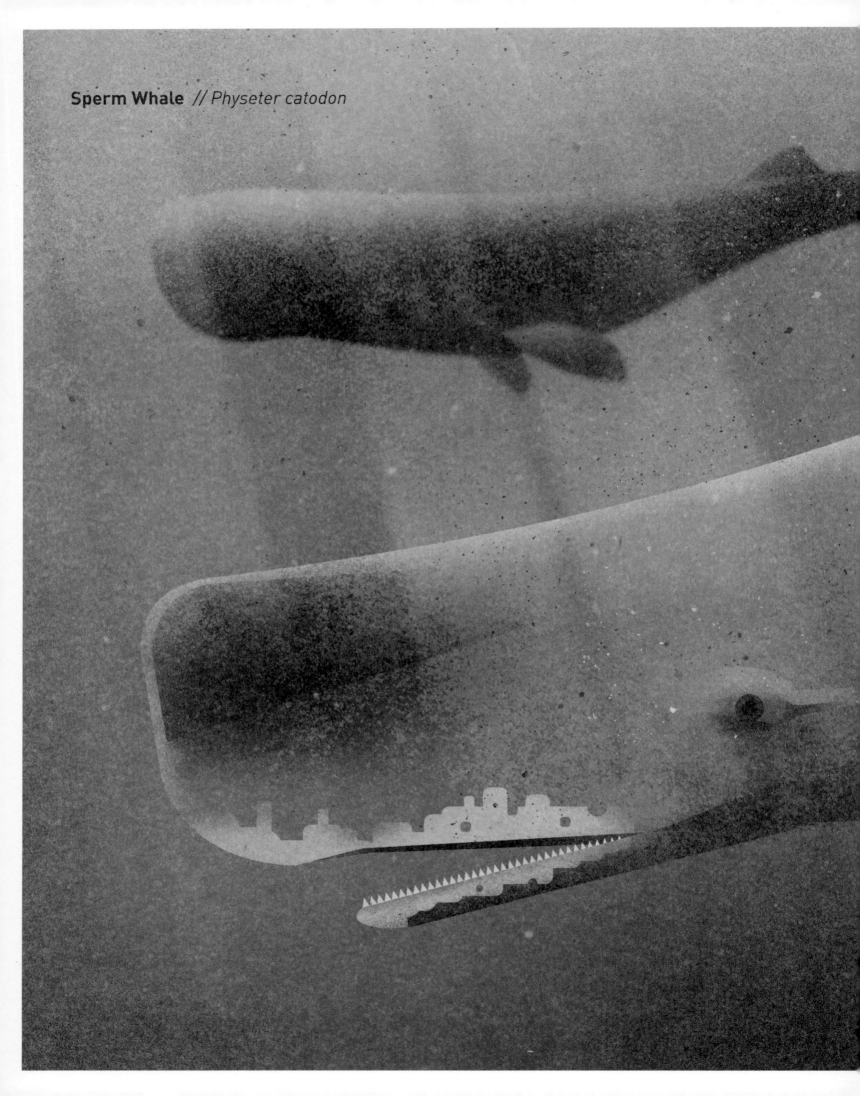

Sperm Whale // *Physeter catodon*

Wolverine // *Gulo gulo*

The largest marten in the world is an extreme athlete and total powerhouse. Not only is the wolverine an excellent swimmer, experienced climber and avid marathon runner, it is also unrivalled in its supreme discipline: the snow sprint. Few animals can match its talents, especially when it comes to eating. When the wolverine's stomach rumbles – which is often – its remarkable set of teeth employ many tonnes of force to crunch up pretty much anything, even bones.

INDEX

NORTH AMERICA // *Region 1*

Puma

Puma concolor // p.8

Bald Eagle

Haliaeetus leucocephalus // p.10

Kodiak Bear

Ursus arctos middendorffi // p.12

Mountain Goat

Oreamnos americanus // p.14

Orca

Orcinus orca // p.16

Polar Bear

Ursus maritimus // p.18

Seal

Phoca vitulina // p. 20

Blue-Footed Booby

Sula nebouxii // p.21

Wolf

Canis lupus // p.22

Chipmunk

Tamias // p.24

Grey Squirrel

Sciurus carolinensis // p.25

Bison

Bison // p.26

American Lobster
Homarus americanus // p.28

Monarch Butterfly
Danaus plexippus // p.30

Texas Rattlesnake
Crotalus atrox // p.32

Coyote
Canis latrans // p.33

Elk
Cervus canadensis // p.34

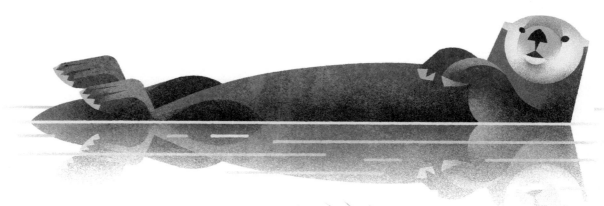

Sea Otter
Enhydra lutris // p.35

Long-Tailed Duck
Clangula hyemalis // p.36

King Eider
Somateria spectabilis // p.37

Striped Skunk
Mephitis mephitis // p.38

Pronghorn Antelope
Antilocapra americana // p.39

Raccoon

Procyon lotor // p.40

Reindeer

Rangifer tarandus // p.42

Canadian Beaver

Castor canadensis // p.44

Long-Tailed Weasel

Mustela frenata // p.46

Turkey

Meleagris gallopavo // p.48

Walrus

Odobenus rosmarus // p.50

Puffin

Fratercula arctica // p.52

Pileated Woodpecker

Dryocopus pileatus // p.49

Red Fox

Vulpes vulpes // p.56

Compass Jellyfish

Chrysaora hysoscella // p.58

Grey Heron

Ardea cinerea // p.59

Roe Deer

Capreolus capreolus // p.60

Barn Owl

Tyto alba // p.62

Squirrel

Sciurus vulgaris // p.64

European Badger

Meles Meles // p.65

White Stork

Ciconia ciconia // p.66

Wild Boar

Sus scrofa // p.68

Hedgehog

Erinaceus europaeus // p.69

White Swan

Cygnus olor // p.70

Black Swan

Cygnus atratus // p.71

Fire Salamander
Salamandra salamandra // p.72

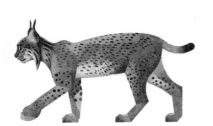

Iberian Lynx
Lynx pardinus // p.74

Peregrine Falcon
Falco peregrinus // p.76

European Mouflon
Ovis orientalis musimon // p.78

Great Spotted Woodpecker
Dendrocopos major Syn Picoides major // S. 79

Brown Hare
Lepus europaeus // p.80

Wood Grouse
Tetrao urogallus // p.82

Red Deer
Cervus elaphus // p.84

Northern Bald Ibis
Geronticus eremita // S. 86

European Bison
Bison bonasus // p.87

Moose
Alces alces // p.88

Crane
Grus grus // p.90

Snow Leopard
Panthera uncia // p.94

Giant Panda
Ailuropoda melanoleuca // p.96

Japanese Macaque
Macaca fuscata // p.98

Great Black Cormorant
Phalacrocorax carbo // p.100

Red Panda
Ailurus fulgens // p.102

Yak
Bos mutus // p.104

Musk deer
Moschidae // p.105

Musk Ox
Ovibos moschatus // p.106

Golden Pheasant
Chrysolophus pictus // p.108

Przewalski's Horse

Equus ferus przewalskii // p.110

Dalmatian Pelican

Pelecanus crispus // p.112

Asian Black Bear

Ursus thibetanus // p.114

Saiga

Saiga tatarica // p.116

Markhor

Capra falconeri // p.117

Alpine Hare

Lepus timidus // p.118

Arctic Fox

Vulpes lagopus // p.118

Ermine

Mustela erminea // p.119

Mandarin Duck

Aix galericulata // p.120

Golden Monkey

Rhinopithecus roxellana // p.121

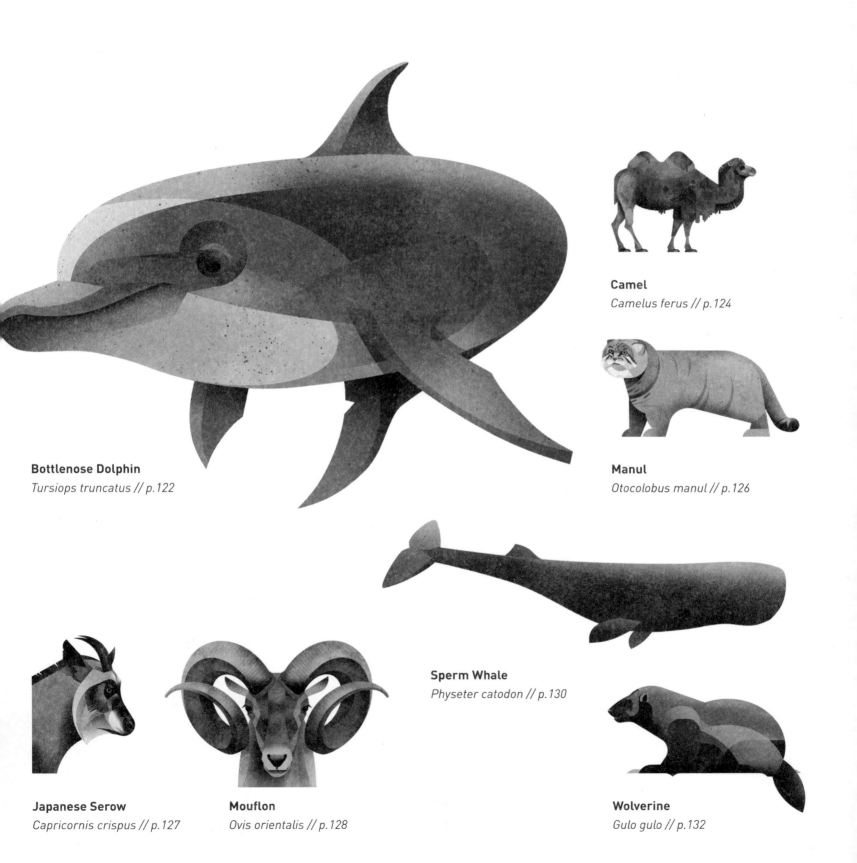

Bottlenose Dolphin
Tursiops truncatus // p.122

Camel
Camelus ferus // p.124

Manul
Otocolobus manul // p.126

Sperm Whale
Physeter catodon // p.130

Japanese Serow
Capricornis crispus // p.127

Mouflon
Ovis orientalis // p.128

Wolverine
Gulo gulo // p.132

My special thanks to Enver Hirsch, Adriane Krakowski and Judith Schüller.

This is a second edition.

Published in 2016 by Flying Eye Books, an imprint of Nobrow Ltd.
27 Westgate Street, London E8 3RL.

Text and Illustration © 2015 Dieter Braun

Translation by Jen Calleja.

Published in the US by Nobrow (US) Inc.
Printed in Turkey

MIX
Paper from
responsible sources
FSC® C126719

ISBN 978-1-909263-96-3
Order from www.flyingeyebooks.com

Coming Soon...
Wild Animals of the South
by Dieter Braun
ISBN 978-1-909263-97-0